Celebrating
Halloween

By: Shelly Nielsen
Illustrated by: Marie-Claude Monchaux

Published by Abdo & Daughters, 6535 Cecilia Circle, Edina, Minnesota 55439.

Library bound edition distributed by Rockbottom Books, Pentagon Tower, P.O. Box 36036, Minneapolis, Minnesota 55435.

2-8-97 JFund 38

Copyright © 1992 by Abdo Consulting Group, Inc., Pentagon Tower, P.O. Box 36036, Minneapolis, Minnesota 55435. International copyrights reserved in all countries. No part of this book may be reproduced in any form without written permission from the publisher. Printed in the United States.

Edited by: Rosemary Wallner

LIBRARY OF CONGRESS CATALOGING-IN-PUBLICATION DATA

Nielsen, Shelly, 1958-
    Halloween / written by Shelly Nielsen; [edited by Rosemary Wallner]
    p. cm. -- (Holiday celebrations)
    Summary: Rhyming text introduces aspects of this annual celebration which occurs on October 31.
    ISBN 1-56239-070-8
    1. Halloween--Juvenile literature. [1. Halloween.] I. Wallner, Rosemary, 1964- II. Title. III. Series:
Nielsen, Shelly, 1958- Holiday celebrations.
GT4965.N54   1992   394.2'683--dc20   91-73031

International Standard Book Number:	**Library of Congress Catalog Card Number:**
1-56239-070-8	91-73031

Celebrating
Halloween

Halloween Is Coming!

When the moon puts on a yellow grin,
and breezes make goosebumps on bare skin,
when birds fly south for warmer places,
and pumpkins put on spooky faces . . .
that's when you can finally say,
"Halloween must be on the way!"

Rustly Leaves

Hold on tight, leaves,
up so high,
waving "hello" from the sky.
You may be pretty —
golden and brown —
but if you don't hold tight,
you'll land on the ground.

Okay, then, leaves,
I warned you.
Now trick-or-treaters
will have leaves to rustle through!

Pumpkin Face

Jack-O'-Lantern,
pumpkin face,
I see you smiling everyplace.
In every window,
on every step —
just what do you think
you're grinning at?

Sometimes you're angry,
with crooked eyes;
Sometimes you're spooky,
with a candle inside.
But always you're grinning that toothy smile.
Why don't you laugh at someone else awhile?

My Jack-O'-Lantern

Every house has a pumpkin,
but mine is unique.
I'm painting a face;
won't that be neat?
Blue for eyes —
round and surprised;
red for lips —
a curve at each tip.
A stroke of bold black
makes a curly moustache.
Not bad, not bad;
looks just like my dad.
Later, when Halloween passes by
my jack-o'-lantern will be
pumpkin pie.

Munchy Seeds

Squish, squish, squish.
Squeezing pumpkin seeds
feels delicious!
They're oozy and slimy
and slippery, too.
When I'm done squishing,
here's what I do:
rinse them and salt them,
spread on a baking sheet —
I bake them till crunchy
at 325 degrees.
When my seeds are cool,
and pumpkin-crunchy
I grab a handful
and munch 'em!

Marie-Claude Ma

Which Costume?

This Halloween,
what will I be?
A movie star?
Pirate?
Chimpanzee?
I try on a wig
and a phony nose;
then a collar, dog ears,
and a plastic bone.
Costume-shopping is so much fun,
I almost hope I'll never be done.

Please look after this Bear. Thank you

claude Tranchand

It's a Parade

Line up! Line up! Single file!
We're having a parade,
Halloween-style.
Ms. Kruse leads us down the hall
wearing our costumes,
one and all.
Pam is a puppy; Todd's a teddy bear;
Terese wears pink curlers in her hair.
And me —
I bet you can't guess.
In my crown, jewels, and gown,
I'm a princess.

Nab an Apple

There's a tub of water
over there,
with apples floating
everywhere.
So close your eyes . . .
gulp a breath . . .
bob for apples, Elizabeth!
Ready now? Get set, don't flub;
Nab an apple —
Glub! Glub! Glub!
Come up for air, dripping wet.
How many apples
did you get?

Who's Afraid?

Who's afraid of a haunted house?
Dusty cobwebs? A squeaky mouse?
Scary pumpkins missing teeth?
Not me! It's fun . . . and make-believe!

So come along; follow me
into the house haunted by my family.
Hold my hand and yell, *"What's that?"*
when you see my sister in a witch's hat.

A haunted house will make you quiver.
You'll see . . .
it's fun to get the shivers.

Safe and Sound

On Halloween,
I'm safe and sound.
I walk with Mom
as we make the rounds.
I look both ways
before crossing the street
and wait to get home
before I eat.
I'm the safest ghost on the road tonight;
but — Boo! — I'm still scary, all right!

Who's That?

"Trick-or-treat, Mrs. Crocker,"
I said when the door opened wide.
Out came my neighbor,
who lives inside.
"Well," said Mrs. Crocker,
"It's a little bumblebee!
You look like Tasheeta;
but how could that be?
She doesn't have wings
or antennae, waving.
I beg your pardon;
I must be mistaken."
She dropped in a treat . . .
and another one, too.
She said, "If you see Tasheeta,
give her this, won't you?"
Then before I could even think,
she said, "Good-bye, sweet bumblebee,"
. . . and winked.

Candy for Everyone

"Ding dong!" rings the bell.

"I'll get it," I yell.

"Trick-or-treat!" the children shout.

"Here's the candy," I say. "Let me give it out."

"Thunk! Thunk!" — the candy lands.

"Thanks, thanks," say my friends.

"Click, click," the door swings shut.

I like giving candy; I'm good at it!

marie-claude monchaux

Candy Count

Gooey chocolate,
Turkish taffy,
Look at my stash of
Halloween candy!
Two orange suckers,
four of red —
("Just one a day," Daddy said).
Malted milk balls,
candy with nuts.
(Too bad I hate nuts — *yuck!*)
Count and count
and count again:
eight sour tarts —
no, ten!
Jawbreakers, caramels,
bubble gum so chewy.
Blow-blow-blow . . .
        KA—BLEWY!

Soap Song

Scrub and rub
in the tub.
Soap that make-up off,
then pull the plug.

Wash away
that orange stain.
Oops!
My clown face
just went down the drain.

Now that I am squeaky clean,
how long, I wonder,
till next Halloween?